Power-of-God-Singing

In The Hebrew New Testament

Janice F. Baca

Hebrew Grammarian and Translator

Power of God Singing
In the Hebrew New Testament

Publisher: Primedia eLaunch LLC

ISBN: 979-8-90119-426-3

 Cover image courtesy of ar.inspiredpencil.com and internal music images by Freepik.com.

Unless otherwise noted, all Scripture quotations are from *The Scriptures* 2009, published by the Institute for Scripture Research (ISR).

Scriptures from the Cochin Hebrew New Testament (Cambridge MS Oo.1.32, Oo.1.16.1, Oo.1.16.2) are translations completed by Janice F. Baca and are part of the publications provided by the Project Truth Ministries team on ProjectTruthMinistries.org.

The book of Revelation is quoted from Janice F. Baca, *The Scroll of Mysteries: Cochin Hebrew Revelation* (Cambridge MS Oo.1.16.1, published in Hondo, TX: independently published, 2024),

For information, contact: ProjectTruthMinistries.org

Table of Contents

Acknowledgements

I'm deeply grateful to Jeff and Miranda Brannon from The Way Remnant ministry, whose encouragement and passion for truth sparked the inspiration to write this paper. What a joy to see this research included in Jeff Brannon's book, *The Priestly Service,* the exciting continuation of *The Priestly Garments: Who We Are In Messiah*. It's amazing to witness how this journey into the Power-of-God-Singing has touched so many hearts—confirming what many have always felt deep inside: that singing in faith truly drives away darkness. Now, with scholarly research to back it up, we can all sing a little louder and bolder!

A special thank you to our dear family friends and gifted musicians, John Reed Austin and Lawrence (LC) Clark, for bringing the Power-of-God-Singing to life through the "Power-of-God-Band." Your music not only filled gatherings with joy but embodied the very heart of the Power-of-God-singing in every note you play.

And to my beloved husband, David Baca—your steadfast love and encouragement have been my anchor throughout this journey. Thank you for believing in me and standing by my side as I share and teach what's in my heart.

\- ***Janice F Baca***

About the Author

Janice F. Baca is a rising prophetic voice, bringing the Spirit and truth of God's word to a more profound understanding, while empowering Yah's people for the end-of-day battles. As a biblical Hebrew grammarian and translator, Janice studied at the Israel Institute of Biblical Studies and pursued graduate studies in Theology. She resides in Hondo, Texas, with her husband, David Baca. Together, Janice and David are voices crying out in the wilderness for the people of Yah to repent, while proclaiming new revelations of Yah's word for the preparations for these end of days. Janice has dedicated many years of her time to research and studies. It is her passion and calling to uncover the hidden mysteries of the Biblical Hebrew grammar.

Janice's prophetic voice is gaining international attention through her translation of *The Scroll of Mysteries: Cochin Hebrew Revelation* and her book, *Demons, Devils, Deities: And The Four Witnesses*. These works collectively explore profound spiritual themes, offering readers a unique perspective on the end of days as foretold by Moses. They illuminate the very days seen by the prophets of old; days filled with the power of God singing! Janice's writing style is characterized by its evocative language and profound insights, drawing readers into a world where ancient wisdom intertwines with contemporary understanding. Her work resonates with those seeking a deeper connection to their connection with Yah and a greater understanding of the mysteries that have captivated humanity for millennia.

For further information on Janice's teachings, video content, and translation initiatives, please visit ProjectTruthMinistries.org. You can also access her YouTube channel at @JaniceFBaca_Translator, as well as the Project Truth Ministries YouTube channel at @ProjectTruthMinistries.

Chapter 1: Spiritual Gift of Power-of-God-Singing

Let me invite you right into the heart of my journey—a journey that I hope will ignite something in you as well. I love to sing to Yehovah, not just because He is worthy, but because I've seen and felt the power that true worship unlocks. When I lift my voice and dance before Elohim (God), it's not as a performance—it's a real encounter. I feel His presence rush in, dissolving my fears and giving me victory over battles I never thought I could win. Here's the most exciting part: this isn't just my story. The same power of song and dance is available for you—especially in these extraordinary times. Worship is so much more than a ritual; it's an invitation for heaven to meet earth in the middle of our everyday struggles. I've experienced deliverance, healing, and breakthrough, and I believe you can too. Sometimes it's hard to describe just how much praise and worship can change a situation, but the Scriptures are filled with stories that show what's possible. Think about Paul and Silas, locked in prison—yet their singing and prayers flung the doors wide open. That's the kind of wonder I want you to discover as you read through my research. Let's step into this adventure together and see what miracles are waiting when we truly sing to Yehovah!

> And at midnight Sha'ul and Silas were praying and singing songs to Elohim, and the prisoners were listening to them. And suddenly a great earthquake took place, so that the foundations of the prison were shaken, **and immediately all the doors were opened and all the chains came loose**. Acts 16:25-26 ISR (emphasis mine)

Additionally, when I read stories like King Jehoshaphat's in Scripture. I can picture the fear and uncertainty that must have gripped Judah as enemies surrounded them. Instead of charging into battle, Jehoshaphat led his people to pray, fast, and—most powerfully—send singers out ahead to praise Elohim! Their worship wasn't just a ritual; it was their weapon. The songs they lifted up brought confusion to the enemy, turning the tide of the battle without anyone even lifting a sword. I imagine the overwhelming relief and joy as Judah gathered the spoils and returned home, knowing they had experienced Elohim's deliverance and peace in a way that could only come through trusting Him and praising with their whole hearts.

> And after consulting with the people, he appointed **those who should sing to יהוה**, and **who should praise the splendour of set-apartness**, as they went out before the army and were saying, "Give thanks to יהוה, for His loving-commitment is everlasting." **And when they began singing and praising, יהוה set ambushes against the children of Ammon, Mo'aḇ, and Mount Sĕʽir, who had come against Yehuḏah, and they were smitten**. 2 Chronicles 20:21-22 ISR (emphasis mine)

Furthermore, Psalm 146:6-9 instructs us that when we exalt Yehovah, it is a weapon like a two-edged sword that takes vengeance on our enemies.

> Let the exaltation of Ĕl be in their mouth, and a two-edged sword in their hand, to execute vengeance on the nations, punishments on the peoples; to bind their sovereigns with chains, and their nobles with iron bands; to execute on them the written right-ruling; a

splendour it is for all His lovingly-committed ones. Praise Yah! Psalm 146:6-9

But before we go any further, I want you to pause for a moment and imagine this: the New Testament lists out an incredible array of spiritual gifts—administration, apostleship, discernment, evangelism, exhortation, faith, giving, healing, helps, hospitality, knowledge, leadership, mercy, prophecy, serving, speaking in tongues, teaching, wisdom—and then, tucked right alongside those, is something absolutely electrifying: power-of-God-singing.[1] Did that surprise you? It surprised me! This isn't just any singing—this is a gift so powerful it was known by King David and the first disciples, but it's been hidden from most of us until now. Can you picture yourself discovering a gift that actually brings the miracles of heaven into the room? When I uncovered this through deep research and ancient Cochin Hebrew New Testament manuscripts, it felt like finding a treasure meant for this exact moment in history—these very days when the world needs Elohim's power more than ever.[2] Just imagine: when you step into power-of-God-singing, you're not just making music—you're releasing a force that can drive out darkness, heal the sick, bring you clarity, and fill your space with God's strength and might. What could happen if you dared to try?

Hebrew Aramaic Lexicons and Dictionaries

Let's take a journey together into the heart of the Hebrew Bible. Have you ever wondered what a word really meant in its original setting? I know I have! When I dig into the Hebrew or Aramaic words in the Tanakh (Old Testament), I often reach for all the best dictionaries and lexicons, hoping to uncover the true meaning behind each word. But honestly, it isn't always straightforward—sometimes, it feels like detective work! Imagine if you and I could travel back in time and ask

---

[1] Spiritual gifts are found in the following verses: 1 Corinthians 12:4-11, 28; Ephesians 4:11-16, and Romans 12:6-8.

[2] Daniel 12:4.

the original authors what they intended. Since we can't, we have to piece it together as best we can. That's why I'm excited to explore the ancient Hebrew root זמר (zayin – mem – resh) with you. Who knows? Maybe what we discover will spark something new—and even help you tap into a bit of "God-power" in your own God-song!

Let's roll up our sleeves and dive into a bit of word detective work together! Have you ever wondered what a single Hebrew word might really mean, or how many layers it could have? I love digging into this kind of mystery, and I want to bring you along for the ride. When I explore the root זמר (zayin – mem – resh), I find myself flipping through pages of brilliant resources like *Gesenius' Hebrew and Chaldee Lexicon to the Old Testament Scriptures*,[3] *Brown Driver Briggs Hebrew and English Lexicon* (BDB),[4] *The Theological Dictionary of the Old Testament* (TDOT),[5] and the *Hebrew, Aramaic Lexicon of the Old*

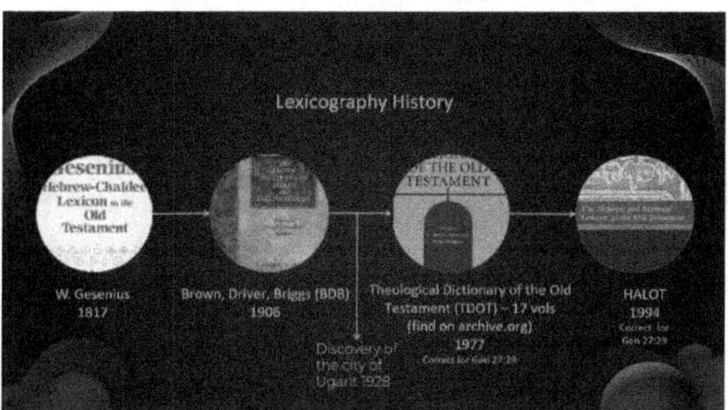

[3] Wilhelm Gesenius and Samuel Prideaux Tregelles. 1979. *Gesenius' Hebrew and Chaldee Lexicon to the Old Testament Scriptures*. Grand Rapids, Mich.: Baker Book House. Copyright.

[4] Brown, Francis, S R Driver, Charles A Briggs, Edward Robinson, James Strong, and Wilhelm Gesenius. 2015. *The Brown, Driver, Briggs Hebrew and English Lexicon: With an Appendix Containing the Biblical Aramaic: Coded with the Numbering System from Strong's Exhaustive Concordance of the Bible*. Peabody, Mass.: Hendrickson Publishers.

[5] G Johannes Botterweck, and Helmer Ringgren. 1980. *Theological Dictionary of the Old Testament*. Grand Rapids, Mich.: William B. Eerdmans Pub. Co. See link for a free download all 17 vols: https://archive.org/details/theological-dictionary-of-the-old-testament/Theological%20Dictionary%20of%20the%20Old%20Testament%20-%2001/

Testament (HALOT).[6] Here's what's fascinating: this one root זמר (zayin – mem – resh), can mean (1) to sing (with or without instruments) and dance, (2) strength or might, and (3) the act of plucking strings, pruning, or cutting down. Isn't it amazing how much richness is packed into a single word? Of course, the search isn't easy—sometimes I wish you and I could hop in a time machine and ask the original writers ourselves! Since we can't, we have to become history detectives, piecing together clues from old dictionaries, ancient manuscripts, and context. It's not an exact science, but that's what makes it so exciting. So, as we go through these discoveries, I hope you'll feel inspired to see how much adventure and meaning can hide in just one ancient word.

To begin, let's step into the fascinating story of Hebrew grammar and linguistics! Instead of a dry review, imagine yourself alongside ancient scribes and storytellers. Did you know that what we call "Hebrew" was once known as the "tongue of Canaan"? In fact, Hebrew and Aramaic began as one language before branching off. The name "Hebrew" itself didn't appear until much later—so much so that even the historian Josephus, writing in the First Century, didn't really distinguish between Hebrew and Aramaic. During King Hezekiah's time, his men referred to their language as "Yudahite" when speaking to the Assyrian invaders (2 Kings 18:26). And in the Assyrian records of that era, the land was called "Yudaea" (Judaea), while the Scriptures describe it as the "tongue of Canaan" (Isaiah 19:18). Even ancient Egypt was sometimes called Canaan![7] Isn't it amazing how language connects us to the past?

---

[6] Ludwig Köhler, and Walter Baumgartner. 2001. *The Hebrew and Aramaic Lexicon of the Old Testament*. Hebrew and Aramaic in contact. In: R. Hasselbach-Andee (Ed.), A companion to Ancient Near Eastern languages. Blackwell.

[7] Ludwig Köhler, and Walter Baumgartner. 2001. *The Hebrew and Aramaic Lexicon of the Old Testament*. Hebrew and Aramaic in contact. In: R. Hasselbach-Andee (Ed.), A companion to Ancient Near Eastern languages, (pp. 439-455). Blackwell.

Now, let's meet an interesting figure in the research of Hebrew study—Heinrich Friedrich Wilhelm Gesenius (1786–1842). Imagine us sitting together, flipping through old books and marveling at the work of a true language detective! The editors of the BDB lexicon even call Gesenius the father of modern Hebrew lexicography. He published his groundbreaking work on Hebrew grammar back in 1817 before turning his attention to the world of dictionaries. Later, the Brown-Driver-Briggs lexicon—maybe you've heard of it?—was published in 1906 and built on Gesenius' earlier work, thanks to editors Francis Brown, Samuel Rolles Driver, and Charles Augustus Briggs. That's why it's called Brown-Driver-Briggs, or BDB for short. It's like a treasure chest of discoveries, but remember, it's only the first stage in our adventure of understanding the language of the Hebrew Bible.

Discovery of the City of Ugarit

Let me take you on a little adventure—a real archaeological treasure hunt! Picture this: it's 1928, a farmer, just doing his daily work, stumbles across an ancient tomb in his field. That single moment sparks a wave of excitement, drawing archaeologists from all over to explore what turns out to be the ancient city of Ugarit, nestled on the northern coast of Syria. Can you imagine the thrill of discovering hundreds of tablets uncovered from the palace and temple ruins? Over 1,500 of these tablets have been published, each one opening a window into a world that peaked between the fifteenth and thirteenth centuries BCE—a time when Ugarit was buzzing with stories and songs.

Let's step into the shoes of an explorer together! Imagine the excitement as archaeologists and locals in Ugarit sifted through the earth and uncovered clay tablets inscribed with a mysterious script (called cuneiform script)—a language the world had never seen before. This language, later known as Ugaritic, was named after the city and proved to be a key that unlocked new secrets about the Hebrew language. Isn't it amazing how ancient discoveries can shine fresh light on something we thought we already understood?

Here's where it gets really personal for us as lovers of language: Ugaritic and Hebrew share many similarities, so these discoveries gave us new ways to understand Hebrew grammar and vocabulary. Let me share one of my favorite linguistic puzzles with you. In Genesis 27:29, there's a word—יִשְׁתַּחֲוּוּ (yish'chavu'u), meaning "to bow down"—that has a rare verb structure called the Hishtafel. For years, the respected Brown Driver Briggs (BDB) lexicon guessed at its origin root, thinking the root was שחה (shin – chet – hey) based on clever letter swapping (called metathesis). But then, thanks to the Ugaritic tablets, scholars discovered this exact verb form and realized the true root was חוי (chet – vav – yod)—a discovery that flipped the old understanding on its head!

This is such a powerful reminder for you and me: even the most celebrated dictionaries are only stepping stones on the journey of discovery. Our understanding continues to grow with every new clue. That's why, when I learned about the misstep in BDB and saw how later resources, such as TDOT and HALOT, corrected it, I felt inspired to question everything I thought I knew about the root זמר (zayin – mem – resh). What hidden depths might we find if we keep exploring together?

Why does this matter for us? Because it reminds us that even the most respected dictionaries and lexicons are really just best guesses—snapshots in an ongoing journey of discovery. This revelation made me rethink everything I thought I knew about the root זמר (zayin – mem – resh). What if, thanks to the spirit of adventure and a willingness to dig deeper, we could uncover an even richer meaning together? Are you ready to see where this exploration takes us?

The Piel Stem System: Intensifier!

Let's dive into something truly fascinating together! I've noticed (and scholars have noticed) that every single verb formed from the root זמר (zayin – mem – resh) in the Hebrew Bible appear*s* in the Piel binyan stem. Why should you care about the Piel stem? Because it's not just any verb form—it's an intensifier! It packs extra energy, intent, and sometimes even a sense of causing something to happen. And here's something fun: even top scholars like Joüon-Muraoka (whose grammar book is still the go-to for Biblical Hebrew) admit that the Piel is mysterious—"the most elusive of the Hebrew conjugations."[8]

So, what does this mean for us as we explore God-singing? It means there's a deeper layer to discover! Let's make it real with an example. Take the Hebrew root שבר (shin – vet – resh). In the basic Qal stem, שָׁבַר (shavar) means, "He broke." No big deal, right? But switch it to the Piel, שִׁבֵּר (shiber), and suddenly it's, "He shattered!" or "He smashed!"—full of passion and intent. Can you picture the difference? He didn't just break it; he meant to, and he did it with all his might!

That's the kind of intensity we're talking about when we see זמר (zayin – mem – resh) in the Piel stem in the Bible. This isn't casual, background singing. This is powerful, purposeful, God-driven singing—done with heart, intention, and maybe even a little bit of holy fire!

Let's keep digging into the Piel stem together! I love how Scholar and Pastor Timothy Smith, in his paper "Review of The Piel Stem System," really brings the text to life by showing us just how many ways the Piel verb stem can be used. Out of the thirty-three uses he lists, I've picked out a few that I think you'll find especially interesting as we explore the root זמר (zayin – mem – resh).

> The 1926 Hebrew Grammar by C.T. Wood and H.C.O. Lanchester (both of Cambridge) briefly states that "the piel usually expresses vigor or eagerness of

[8] Joüon, Paul, and Takamitsu Muraoka. 2005. *A Grammar of Biblical Hebrew*. Roma: Ed. Pontificio Istituto Biblico, 140.

action" (p. 72) but later adds that "the piel is frequently causative, especially in stative verbs; e.g., 'he caused to learn,' i.e., taught." (p. 73).

...After a search of ten Hebrew Grammars, Rosenthal's Aramaic Grammar, and a Syriac Grammar for comparison, I have compiled a list of (33) the following uses for the piel..."[9]

Three of the 33 uses quoted are:

20. Multiple subjects in the same act

21. Multiple objects of the same act

22. Multiple occurrences of the same act.

I've gathered a treasure trove of examples. I can't wait to share some of these discoveries with you as we dive into how the Piel brings powerful meaning to God-singing!

What truly excites me is discovering how the Tanakh habitually uses the Piel verb stem for זמר (zayin – mem – resh) with such intention and divine purpose. It feels as if the language itself is reaching out, urging us to see that this word isn't just about singing, strength, or even plucking strings—it's all of those, supercharged with passion and meaning! I can't help but smile at how the Piel verb stem cranks up each meaning, making the experience of God-singing feel so alive and deliberate. It's like the text invites us to join in—singing with all our heart and purpose.

So, when I dig into these words, I'm not just looking at their history—I'm searching for the deeper story the context and verb stem reveal. And honestly, my curiosity only grew after conversations with my Biblical Hebrew professor (who's also a Cohen in Jerusalem!) and after exploring the Cochin Hebrew New Testament manuscripts (Cambridge MS Oo.1.32, Oo.1.16.1, Oo.1.16.2). Their insights made me stop

[9] Smith, Timothy. 2019. "Review of The Piel Stem System." River Valley Conference of the Minnesota District, February 2019, 6-8.

and wonder: What powerful message might be waiting for us when we look at the root זמר (zayin – mem – resh) through this lens of intensity and purpose? Let's unpack this together!

Power-of-God-Singing Described by a Cohen?

Let me take you into a moment that sparked my curiosity and changed the way I see the word זִמְרָת (zimrat). Picture me sitting in my Biblical Hebrew Course at the Israel Institute of Biblical Studies, listening intently as my Cohen instructor shared something that made my eyes light up. He explained that זִמְרָת—the ancient, Piel form of the word זמר (zayin – mem – resh)—might mean so much more than just "singing." What if it's actually "Power-of-God singing," or as he called it, "God-singing"? Imagine: music so filled with divine strength that it's not just a song, but a force!

If that's true, then all those old etymological roots—(1) Song, (2) Might, and even (3) Pruning or Cutting down—aren't just definitions, but are woven together into something alive and powerful. I got even more excited when I came across Chaim Bentorah's word study, which suggests זמר (zayin – mem – resh) could mean a song that literally cut down your enemies! Suddenly, these ideas weren't just theories—they felt like an invitation to discover something miraculous.

That's why I've been digging through the Tanakh and the Cochin Hebrew New Testament manuscripts with new eyes and a fresh sense of wonder. What if this unique, miracle-filled singing is especially important for the end of days, when the one hundred forty-four thousand will sing a mysterious song that only they can learn? I'd love for you to imagine this with me: What would it mean for you to step into the power of God-singing in your own life?

God-Singing in the Tanakh (Old Testament)

In Exodus 15:2, written in Ancient Hebrew, we find the archaic form of the root זמר (zayin – mem – resh) as זִמְרָת

(zimrat, H2176)[10] in the Song of the Sea (Exodus 15:2). Thus, if we apply the theories that the etymological root זמר (zayin – mem - resh) means God-singing with music and dance, or cutting down our enemies in the song, then the Song of the Sea is a song of victory and may even be a war song that exhibits great power when sung! Additionally, the Song of the Sea is the first and oldest song in the Tanakh, and it is my theory that it may also be the final song sung at the end of days because Yehovah is the first and the last[11] and His song is first and will also be His last. And the first song may also be the final song sung through the one hundred forty-four thousand in Revelation 14. To further complicate matters, there appear to be missing verses that have been discovered in the Song of the Sea in Exodus 15 within the Dead Sea Scrolls (DSS).[12] And this could be the reason why others cannot learn the song, for these could be the verses that have been long lost from the ancient of days. For if this is indeed the song of the one hundred and forty-four thousand, then the words, tune, and frequency must be imparted to the one hundred forty-four thousand miraculously at the end of days. Therefore, it is for these reasons, and many others, that I believe the song of the one hundred forty-four thousand will be the renewed Song of the Sea because it is the final song to be sung in the latter days!

---

[10] The Archaic form is also found in Exodus 15:2, Psalm 118:14, and Isaiah 12:2.

[11] Chaim Bentorah. 2023. "Hebrew Word Study – a Pruning Praise – Zamar - Chaim Bentorah." Chaim Bentorah. April 5, 2023.

https://www.chaimbentorah.com/2023/04/hebrew-word-study-a-pruning-praise-zamar/.

[12] George J. Brooke, "Power to the Powerless—A Long-Lost Song of Miriam," *Biblical Archaeology Review* 20 (1994): 62–65. The Miriam fragment is published in Sidnie A. White, "4Q364 and 365: A Preliminary Report," in The Madrid Qumran Conference, eds. J. Trebolle Barrera and L. Vegas Montaner, Studies in the Text of the Desert of Judah 11 (Leiden: Brill; Madrid: Editorial Complutense, 1992), 217–228 [222–224].

Chapter 2: King David, The God-Singer

Let me bring you into one of my favorite stories—King David truly grasped the life-changing power of praise and worship. For him, singing wasn't just about melodies; it was spiritual warfare, something I like to call God-singing. Picture young David, harp in hand, called to King Saul's side because Saul was plagued by tormenting spirits sent to him by Yehovah for his disobedience. I always imagine the tension in that room. The air must have felt heavy until David began to play. His music didn't just entertain—it brought real peace and relief, driving away those dark spirits, just as 1 Samuel 16:23 describes. That's the kind of miraculous impact God-singing can have!

> And the Spirit of יהוה turned aside from Sha'ul, and an evil spirit from יהוה troubled him. and the servants of Sha'ul said to him, "Look, now, an evil spirit from Elohim is troubling you. Please, let our master command your servants who are before you, to seek out a man who is a skilled player on the lyre. And it shall be that when the evil spirit from Elohim is upon you, that he shall play with his hand, and you be well. And Sha'ul said to his servants, "Please get me a man that plays well, and bring him to me." And one of the servants answered and said, "Look, I have seen a son of Yishai the Bĕyth Leḥemite, **who knows how to**

> **play, a brave one, and a man of battle, and skilled in words, and a handsome man. And יהוה is with him.**" 1 Samuel 16:14-18 ISR (emphasis mine)

> And it came to be, whenever the *evil* spirit from Elohim was upon Sha'ul, that Dawiḏ would take a lyre and play it with his hand. **Then Sha'ul would become refreshed and well, and the evil spirit would leave him**. 1 Samuel 16:23 ISR (emphasis mine)

I love how 2 Samuel 23:1 calls King David the "sweet God-singer of Israel" (זְמִרוֹת zimrat, from the root זמר (zayin – mem – resh)). That phrase jumps off the page for me because it recognizes David's one-of-a-kind, miraculous spiritual gift. It's like Scripture is inviting us to see David not just as a king or warrior, but as someone who sang so powerfully to Elohim that it became part of his identity—and maybe, if we let it, become part of ours too.

> And these are the last words of Dawiḏ, the saying of Dawiḏ son of Yishai, the saying of the man raised above, the anointed of the Elohim of Ya'aqob, and the sweet **God-singer** (זְמִרוֹת zimrat) **of Yisra'ěl**: (2 Samuel 23:1 ISR (emphasis [and addition] mine)

I can't help but feel inspired when I think about King David recognizing his miraculous gift from Yehovah. Imagine him pouring his heart into the Psalms—those *mizmorim*[13]—which I truly believe are God-songs written as a legacy for all future generations of God-singers like you and me. It's a little sad to realize that many English translations leave out the special introductions to these *mizmorim*. Those opening lines often call out to the chief Musician, inviting everyone to get ready for a power-of-God-song, like in Psalm 20:1. Can you

[13] Mizmorim Psalms are as follows: Psalm 1, 3, 4, 5, 6, 8, 9, 12, 13, 15, 19, 20, 21, 22, 23, 24, 29, 30, 31, 38, 39, 40, 41, 47, 48, 49, 50, 51, 62, 63, 64, 65, 66, 67, 68, 75, 75, 76, 77, 79, 82, 83, 84, 85, 87, 88, 92, 98, 100, 101, 108, 110, 139, 140, 141, 143.

picture the anticipation building before the music even begins?

> To the chief Musician, A **Psalm** (מזמור mizmor) of David. (Psalms 20:1 ISR (emphasis [and addition] mine))

Let me invite you to imagine King David not just as a king or a poet, but as a master strategist whose weapon was worship! I love picturing him, the sweet God-singer, fully convinced that singing to Yehovah could cut down his enemies and turn the tide of battle. I'm struck by how he didn't just keep this gift to himself—he organized whole teams of singers and musicians, setting them in place as a kind of spiritual army. Can you picture the energy and faith it took to send singers ahead as part of a military campaign, like in 1 Chronicles 25:1? Or to call everyone together to lift up praises before Elohim, as in 1 Chronicles 15:16 and 24?

What amazes me even more is that David involved his military commanders, instructing them to help appoint families of worshipers—people like Asaph, Heman, and Jeduthun—to sing and prophesy as an actual military duty, a God-given assignment. That's how much David believed in the miraculous power of God-singing. I wonder what would happen if we approached worship with the same passion and expectancy—that when we sing, Yehovah's power fills the place and changes everything!

> And Dawiḏ spoke to the leaders of the Lĕwites to appoint their brothers the singers with instruments of song, harps, and lyres, and cymbals, to lift up the voice with joy. (1 Chronicles 15:16 ISR)

> And Dawiḏ and the commanders of the army separated for the service some of the sons of Asaph, and of Hĕman, and of Yeḏuthun, **who should prophesy with lyres, with harps, and with cymbals**, 1 Chronicles 25:1a ISR (emphasis mine))

What really excites me is how several Psalms actually invite us—yes, you and me—to step into God-singing ourselves. When I read verses like Psalm 81:2, Psalm 98:5, Psalm 147:1, and Psalm 149:3, I feel as though Scripture is calling us to join a chorus of worshipers across generations, lifting our voices with passion and purpose. Can you imagine the joy of adding your own God-song to that ancient, powerful melody?

> Lift up a **God song** (זִמְרָה – zimra) and beat the tambourine, the pleasant lyre, and with the harp." (Psalms 81:2 ISR (emphasis [and Hebrew addition] mine))
>
> **God-Sing** (זַמְּרוּ -zamru) to Yehovah with the lyre, with the lyre and the voice of a God song (זִמְרָה - zimra)," (Psalms 98:5 ISR (emphasis [and addition] mine))
>
> "Praise Yah! For it is good to **God-sing** (זַמְּרָה -zamra) praises to our Elohim. For it is pleasant – praise is fitting." (Psalms 147:1 ISR (emphasis [and addition] mine))
>
> "Let them praise His Name in a dance; Let them **God-sing** (יְזַמְּרוּ - yezamru) praises to Him with the tambourine and lyre." (Psalms 149:3 ISR (emphasis [and addition] mine))

I find it so inspiring that King David set an example not just for his own time but for us, too—especially for those of us living in these challenging and dark days. He didn't see God-singing as something optional or merely uplifting; he saw it as a vital spiritual weapon! When David played and sang before King Saul, the darkness had to retreat—demons literally fled. That wasn't just a story for the past; I truly believe this is meant for us now. Imagine what could happen if we approached God-singing with the same faith and expectation. When we lift our voices to Yehovah, we can believe for victory, deliverance, and healing to break through in our own lives and in the world around us.

Chapter 3: The Chief Prevailer!

Let me invite you into the story behind King David—a power-of-God singer, a warrior, and a musician whose songs have inspired generation after generation. When I think about the מזמורים mizmorim (plural form of the mizmor, Power-of-God-song) of the Psalms, I see so much more than ancient poetry. David's music was a declaration of victory! He used unique language, not just to celebrate, but to paint the music leader—the chief musician—as a true prevailer (root: נצח – nun- tsade- chet). Imagine that: the person leading the worship wasn't just keeping everyone in tune, but was leading the people into victory through the power of song! Wait… What? Is the Chief Musician more than a leader of music?

Here's something I want to share from my own journey of study: I used to overlook the value of older lexicons and dictionaries, but I've learned that every resource has something to offer. Take BDB, for example—it references Jerome, an early theologian who suggested that "choirmaster" (root נצח (nun – tsade – chet)), could be better understood as "the overcomer," "victorious," or "prevailer." That gives the phrase "to the chief Musician…" in Psalm 20:1 a whole new depth of understanding. It's not just about music; it's about overcoming, about victory! And when I read that Eusebius and

Theodocia thought this idea might be especially important for the end of days,[14] I couldn't help but agree. What if Yehovah is inviting us, right now, to become prevailers through the power of God-music?

> To the Chief Musician, A **Psalm** (מזמור mizmor) of David. (Psalms 20:1 ISR (emphasis [and addition] mine))

Additionally, I love how the story of the prophet Habakkuk, writing around 612 BCE just before the Babylonian invasion, feels so relatable—he moves from wrestling with questions and doubts to boldly expressing faith in Yehovah's power and deliverance. What really stands out to me is how Habakkuk 3 uses the root נצח (nun – tsade – chet), the same word for "prevailer," in verse 19. The final line could even be translated as, "For the prevailer *(לַמְנַצֵּחַ בִּנְגִינוֹתָי)* on my stringed instruments!" I can just picture Habakkuk leading with his song, prevailing through music—an encouragement for you and me that our own songs of faith can shift the atmosphere and lead to victory, even in the toughest moments.

If מְנַצֵּחַ (menatzeach, root: נצח (nun – tsade – chet)), is describing a leader who is not only a leader of music, but also describes an overcomer *with or through* music, then the leading overcomer will guide the people to ultimate victory at the end of days – including overcoming the dragon and the beast described in Revelation 12 and 13, including overcoming the demonic! And I believe that Psalm 91 is key to victory and should be prayed, proclaimed, and even sung every day![15]

---

[14] Brown, Francis, S R Driver, Charles A Briggs, Edward Robinson, James Strong, and Wilhelm Gesenius. 2015, 664. *The Brown, Driver, Briggs Hebrew and English Lexicon: With an Appendix Containing the Biblical Aramaic: Coded with the Numbering System from Strong's Exhaustive Concordance of the Bible*. Peabody, Mass.: Hendrickson Publishers.

[15] Baca, Janice F. 2024. *Demons, Devils, Deities: And The Four Witnesses*. Hondo, Texas.

As I wrap up this journey with you, I want to share just how much I've come to appreciate the treasure hunt of exploring lexicons, dictionaries, and every detail of Biblical Hebrew. Each word feels like a clue in an unfolding mystery! If Jerome is right about the root נצח (nun, tsade, chet) pointing to a "lead prevailer," and if Eusebius and Theodocia are onto something, then maybe you and I are being invited to rediscover a powerful, overlooked spiritual gift for our own time. What if the power-of-God-music is meant for us—right now, in these days? I hope this inspires you to dig deeper, ask bold questions, and seek out the spiritual gifts that can bring victory and hope in your own life!

Chapter 4: Power Singers in the Hebrew New Testament

Imagine holding in your hands a piece of history: the Cochin Hebrew New Testament (Cambridge MS Oo.1.32, Oo.1.16.1, Oo.1.16.2), discovered in Cochin, India, by Claudius Buchanan in 1803 in the synagogue of the Malabari Black Jews. While the manuscript may be imperfect, it is nothing short of remarkable—a treasure that has captivated scholars and readers around the world. What makes it so fascinating is its unique blend of late Second Temple Hebrew grammar with Mishnaic Hebrew and Aramaic influences, setting it apart from any other known Hebrew New Testament manuscripts. Even more intriguing are its Tanakh (Old Testament) references, especially the distinct use of the word זמר (zayin – mem – resh). As you explore the manuscript's verses, you'll notice the deliberate choice to highlight a very specific kind of singing. The authors wanted their readers—not just to read, but to feel and understand—the subtle differences between each type of song. If we follow their lead and apply the same verb stem found in the Tanakh, we can see that every instance of the word זמר (zayin – mem – resh) in the Cochin Hebrew New Testament appears in the Piel verb stem, hinting at a singing that is both intentional and full of passion.

But before we dive deeper, take a moment to notice how the Cochin Hebrew New Testament thoughtfully distinguishes between singing and praising in its translations of Cochin Hebrew Matthew 11:17 and Acts 16:25. In Cochin Hebrew Matthew 11:17, the phrase is simple and direct: "We sing" (שיר – shir). In contrast, Cochin Hebrew Acts 16:25 describes Paul and Silas as praying and "praising." The choice of words here isn't arbitrary—it invites you to picture the scene vividly, to sense the difference between casual singing and heartfelt praise. This distinction isn't about singing to God with intensity or intention; it's about painting a nuanced, living image of these moments for every reader.

> and they say, 'We sing (שירים – shirim) for you and you are not dancing. And we lament (קוננים - konnim) for you, but you do not weep." (Cochin Matthew 11:17 (emphasis [and Hebrew addition] mine))

> And in the middle of the night, Paul and Silas were praying and praising (משבחים – meshabchim) Elodim (God), and prisoners were listening to them. (Cochin Acts 16:25 (emphasis [and addition] mine))

Now, picture yourself among the first readers of the Cochin Hebrew New Testament, encountering verses that celebrate the spiritual gift of the God-song. These passages don't just tell; they urge the community to find strength in the power of a God-song and to truly prove themselves through God-singing. You can feel the difference—this isn't the everyday singing mentioned in Cochin Hebrew Matthew 11:17 or Acts 16:25. Instead, as you read Colossians 3:16 in this manuscript, you're invited into a type of singing that, through the Piel verb stem, bursts forth with intention and intensity. It's as if the manuscript is calling you to join in, to sing with passion and purpose.

> And speak to your soul in a God-song (מזמור – mizmor) and praise. And sing God songs (מזמרים – mizmorim) being in the Spirit." Cochin Hebrew

> Ephesians 5:19 (emphasis [and Hebrew addition] mine)
>
> And let the word of the Messiah dwell in your sons in all wisdom, and learn proving yourselves with singings (שירות – shirot) and praises (תושבחות – teshveachot), and (intensely and intentionally) God-singing (מזמרים – mezamrim) to the Lord in your hearts." Cochin Hebrew Colossians 3:16 (emphasis [and Hebrew addition] mine)

Next, imagine the scene in Cochin Hebrew Luke 15:25: the prodigal son returns home, and the air is alive with more than just praise—there's an eruption of God-Singing, a joyful celebration that fills every corner of the house. You can almost hear the music and feel the embrace of a family reunited. In these moments, the singing becomes more than intense; it transforms into a Piel causative singing, a sound that embodies the deep love Yehovah holds between parents and their children. Through this God-singing, we're invited to glimpse how Yehovah Himself rejoices and loves when His lost children find their way back to Him.

> And the eldest son was in the city. And then he came towards the house, and he heard great sound (intense and intentional) God-singing (זמר – zemer). (Cochin Hebrew Luke 15:25 (emphasis [and Hebrew addition] mine))

Now, imagine hearing the words of Cochin Hebrew Romans 15:9 as if they're spoken directly to you: even when we find ourselves scattered among the nations, we're called to lift our voices and God-sing to the name of Yehovah. No matter where we are, this invitation remains—a personal call to join in a song that unites us across every distance.

> And the nations will praise Yehovah for the substitution of mercy upon them as it is written, 'I will give thanks to You in the nations, and I will (intensely and intentionally, continually) God-sing (אזמר – azamer) to Your name!'" Cochin Hebrew Romans 15:9 (emphasis [and Hebrew addition] mine)

Let's pause and listen closely to Cochin Hebrew 1 Corinthians 14:15. Here, Paul isn't just instructing—he's inviting each of us to discover and use our miraculous spiritual gifts with real understanding, especially the gift of God-singing. Imagine being told that when you sing to God, you're tapping into something truly miraculous—a unique gift from Elohim Himself. This isn't just music; it's an act of worship infused with power and might. So the next time you lift your voice in song, remember: you're participating in something extraordinary, a spiritual gift that connects you directly to the divine.

> What now I do is pray in the spirit and pray in understanding. And what I God-sing (מזמר – mezamer) in the Spirit, I will (intensely and intentionally, continually) God-sing (אזמר – azamer) with understanding.'" Cochin Hebrew 1 Corinthians 14:15 (emphasis [and Hebrew addition] mine)

Now, imagine gathering with others and letting the miracle gift of God-singing flow through you, just as Cochin Hebrew 1 Corinthians 14:26 encourages. Your voice, joined with others, becomes a source of strength and encouragement—a living expression of faith that uplifts everyone present.

> I say now, my brothers, that truly as you gather together, those of you who have a God-song (מזמור – mizmor), or an utterance; or if there is a word of knowledge, or an interpretation: let all this be to build them." (Cochin Hebrew 1 Corinthians 14:26 (emphasis [and Hebrew addition] mine))

Picture your faith as gold, tested and refined by fire. That's the powerful image 1 Peter paints in Cochin Hebrew 1 Peter 1:7—our most challenging moments, our trials, can be transformed into a God-song. In the midst of refining, you're invited to find hope and beauty, letting your own God-song rise from the very heart of perseverance.

> So that we may find your faith more honest than silver refined by fire, to (intensely, intentionally, continually) God-sing (זמר – zamer) and praise; and to praise when the day Yeshua Messiah is discovered." (Cochin Hebrew 1 Peter 1:7 (emphasis [and Hebrew addition] mine))

Now, imagine the wisdom found in Cochin Hebrew James: when your heart is full of goodness and joy, God-singing isn't just encouraged—it's essential. The text uses the word (צריך – tzarich), meaning "need, should, must; necessary, required." It's as if the manuscript is gently reminding you that if your heart overflows with kindness, positivity, or gratitude, then singing to Elohim is not just an option, but a beautiful necessity. Your joyful heart naturally finds its voice in a song to the Divine.

> And if one of you suffers anything, he must (צריך – tzarich) pray. And if one among you is of good heart, he must (צריך - tzarich) (intentionally and intensely, continually) God-sing (לזמר – lezamer) psalms." Cochin Hebrew James 5:13 (emphasis [and Hebrew addition] mine)

Chapter 5: The End of Day God-Singers

Imagine yourself stepping into the world of *The Scroll of Mysteries: Cochin Hebrew Revelation.*[16] Here, you stand among three extraordinary groups of God-singers in the latter days: the twenty-four elders, the one hundred forty-four thousand, and those courageous souls who overcome the dragon and the beast—could you be counted among them? In these times of trials, battles, and troubles, the music is anything but ordinary. The text hints that these verses are filled with the זמר (zayin – mem – resh) Piel verb stem, painting a vivid picture of singing that is intentional, intense, and sometimes even unstoppable. It's a call not just to sing, but to pour your heart into every note—perhaps even to find yourself singing continually, carried by the passion of faith.

> And they (intensely and intentionally, continually) God-sang (זמרו - zimru) a renewed song and said, "You are worthy to take the scroll and open its seals, for You were slain, and You redeemed us by Your own blood." (Cochin Hebrew Revelation 5:9 (emphasis [and Hebrew addition] mine))

[16] Baca, Janice. 2024. *The Scroll of Mysteries: Cochin Hebrew Revelation.* Second Edition. Hondo, Texas.

> They were (intensely and intentionally) God-singing (מזמרים - mezamrim) the renewed song before the throne, the four living creatures, and the elders. No one was able to learn this song but the hundred and forty-four thousand that He redeemed from the ground." (Cochin Hebrew Revelation 14:3 (emphasis [and Hebrew addition] mine))

> They (intensely, and intentionally, continually) God-sang (מזמרים - mezamrim) the song of Moses and the song of the Lamb, saying, 'Great are the works of Yehovah, Elohim of Armies! Justice and truth are your ways, King of kings!' (Cochin Hebrew Revelation 15:3 (emphasis [and Hebrew addition] mine))

Imagine facing the end of days—not just as a distant prophecy, but as a real, looming challenge that will test every ounce of your faith and courage. In these extraordinary times, survival alone isn't enough; we're called to overcome with the miraculous gifts Elohim provides. Picture Yehovah's people, you included, relying on the miracle gifts of the Holy Spirit—not just to endure, but to become a beacon for others in the darkest moments. This is why miraculous God-singing isn't just a spiritual extra; it's an essential weapon in the final battle. Through this gift, we find strength for healing, deliverance, clarity of mind, and even victories that go far beyond the battlefield. When the days grow severe, let your God-song rise—it just might be the miracle you and those around you need most.

Chapter 6: Other Hebrew New Testament Manuscripts

As we come to the end of this journey, I invite you to marvel with me at the uniqueness of the Cochin Hebrew New Testament manuscripts (Cambridge MS Oo.1.32, Oo.1.16.1, Oo.1.16.2). My curiosity led me to dive deep into a comparative analysis with other Hebrew New Testament manuscripts, zeroing in on the powerful word root זמר (zayin – mem – resh) across several key verses: Luke 15:25, Romans 15:9, Ephesians 5:19, Colossians 3:16, 1 Corinthians 14:15, 26, 1 Peter 1:7, James 5:13, and Revelation 5:9, 14:3, 15:3. What follows is not just a list, but the story of what makes this manuscript so extraordinary—a glimpse into the spiritual and linguistic treasures.

Paris 131[17] (Bibliothèque Sainte-Geneviève, MS. 131)

Luke 15:25: Yes, זמר (zayin – mem – resh) does appear, but it is used as a noun and not as a verb.

[17] "Paris. Bibliothèque Sainte-Geneviève, Ms. 131 | Biblissima." 2025. Biblissima.fr. 2025. https://portail.biblissima.fr/en/ark:/43093/mdata62ef2966f5fc2ec579d00a3175d46415cad214d0.

Romans 15:9: Yes, זמר (zayin – mem – resh) does appear as a verb.

1 Corinthians 14:15: Yes, זמר (zayin – mem – resh) does appear, but used in a different verb stem.

1 Corinthians 14:26: Yes, זמר (zayin – mem – resh) does appear as a verb.

Ephesians 5:19: Yes, זמר (zayin – mem – resh) does appear, but only used once as a verb and not as a noun.

Colossians 3:16: No, this word does not appear in this text.

James 5:13: Yes, זמר (zayin – mem – resh) does appear, but uses a different verb form than the Cochin Hebrew James.

Special Note: The Paris 131 is a Hebrew New Testament manuscript gifted to Pope Clement VIII and is a translation from Greek to Hebrew with some modifications.

The Hebrew Gospels of Catalonia Vat. ebr. 100[18]

Luke 15:25: No, זמר (zayin – mem – resh) does not appear in this text.

Special Note: The Hebrew Gospels of Catalonia contain only Matthew, Mark, Luke, and John and are translations from the Catalan language into Hebrew.[19]

The Freiburg HS-314[20] New Testament

No, זמר (zayin – mem – resh) does not appear on all accounts.

---

[18] "DigiVatLib." 2025. Vatlib.it. 2025. https://digi.vatlib.it/view/MSS_Vat.ebr.100/0007.

[19] Hames, Harvey J. 2012. "Translated from Catalan: Looking at a Fifteenth-Century Hebrew Version of the Gospels," January, 285–302.

[20] "Neues Testament in Hebräischer Übersetzung ([S. L.], 1563) (Universitätsbibliothek Freiburg I. Br., Hs. 314) - Digital Collections

Special Note: The Frieburg HS-314 is a nearly word-for-word translation from Greek to Hebrew.

The Manchester Gaster 1616[21] New Testament

Yes, זמר (zayin – mem – resh) does appear in all accounts, because it is a copy of the Cochin Hebrew New Testament.

Special Note: The Manchester Gaster 1616 is a corrupted copy of the Cochin Hebrew New Testament (Cambridge MS Oo.1.32, Oo.1.16.1, and Oo.1.16.2). The scribe included many marginal notes and made random changes, including removing most of the written names of Yehovah.

The Marseille MS 24[22] New Testament

Luke 15:24: No, זמר (zayin – mem – resh) does not appear.

Special Note: This manuscript contains Luke and Acts only.

The Shepreve [23] New Testament

James 5:13: Yes, זמר (zayin – mem – resh) does appear, but uses a different verb structure form from the Cochin Hebrew James.

Special Note: This manuscript is part of the collection of the British Royal Museum in *London, Roy MS 16 A II.* This manuscript was donated to the Museum by King George II as part of a group of manuscripts referred to as the 'Old Royal Library.' This handwritten manuscript was presented to King

Freiburg - University Library Freiburg." 2025. Uni-Freiburg.de. 2025. https://dl.ub.uni-freiburg.de/diglit/hs314?ui_lang=eng.

[21] "Neues Testament in Hebräischer Übersetzung ([S. L.], 1563) (Universitätsbibliothek Freiburg I. Br., Hs. 314) - Digital Collections Freiburg - University Library Freiburg." 2025. Uni-Freiburg.de. 2025. https://dl.ub.uni-freiburg.de/diglit/hs314?ui_lang=eng.

[22] Municipal Archives of Marseille, Marseille, France Ms. 48.

[23] British Royal Museum in London, Royal MS 16 A II.

Henry VIII by John Shepreve, a noted Hebrew scholar at Corpus Christi College, Oxford University.[24]

[24] Jones, M. 2021. *The Epistle of James (Ya'akov): A Translation from the Hebrew*. Edited by Pam Lutzker and Jonathan Felt. Kerrville, Texas: B'nai Emunah Institute for Accelerated Learning, 10.

Chapter 7: Final Thoughts

Many of us knew in our hearts that singing praises to our Elohim would bring about victory and the destruction of our enemies, but our theory lacked academic evidence. However, this booklet, "Power of God Singing: In the Hebrew New Testament," gives great confidence to worshipers everywhere.

Oh, it is so amazing! The results of this comparative analysis are nothing short of electrifying: the Cochin Hebrew New Testament (Cambridge MS Oo.1.32, Oo.1.16.1, Oo.1.16.2) is in a league of its own! No other Hebrew New Testament manuscript on earth contains all the powerful Hebrew markers of the unique זמר (zayin – mem – resh)—the intense and intentional power-of-God-singing, expressed with the thrilling Piel verb stem. Imagine uncovering a manuscript that connects you directly to the epic worship of King David himself! These ancient words invite you to experience worship as a force so dynamic and purposeful that it echoes through the ages. This is your invitation: reflect on the extraordinary teachings of the Cochin Hebrew New Testament and boldly ask Yehovah for the gift of God-singing. When you step into this power, you're not just singing—you're driving away darkness, unlocking healing, and clearing your mind with every note. Don't wait—embrace this day, lift your voice, and God-sing to Yehovah with all your heart!

- ***Janice F Baca***

Chapter 8: The Covenant with Yehovah

Imagine setting out on a journey with 33 others, your heart pounding with anticipation, as you cross the ancient landscapes of Saudi Arabia in search of the mysteries of Mount Sinai. This wasn't just another trip—it was an expedition to uncover the evidence of the exodus and walk where Moses and the children of Israel once stood. On the final day, excitement and awe filled the air as the group hiked to the very altar Moses had built, preparing to enter into a covenant with Yehovah, just as their ancestors had 3,500 years ago. But this time, there was a beautiful difference—the covenant meal would be shared in memory of Yeshua, honoring His words from 1 Corinthians 11:24.

The expeditioners brought with them juice and crackers representing the covenant meal, along with a handwritten Ketubah for each member of the party to sign and witness their covenant agreement with Yehovah.

The Original Covenant

Picture yourself standing among the children of Israel, 3,500 years ago, as Yehovah offers a life-changing covenant—a sacred invitation to hear and obey His Voice. Imagine the awe and trembling in the camp, the promise echoing through the generations. Yet, despite this divine offer, the people hesitated, turning away from the Voice that called them (see Deuteronomy 5:22-29). The weight of the covenant was sealed in blood (Exodus 24:3-8), a dramatic moment of commitment and consequence. But as history unfolded, the people broke the covenant, facing the ultimate penalty (Exodus 32:1-8). In an act of mercy, Yehovah provided a way out—a substitute through the sacrifice of animals for their sins (Leviticus 17:11; Hebrews 9:7). Then, in the most profound act of love, Yeshua stepped in and paid the price with His own blood, not only for Israel but for the whole world (Isaiah 53:5; 12-15). Let that truth sink in: you are part of this incredible story of redemption and hope.

Chapter 9: Ketubah

Imagine the significance: centuries after Moses, Rabbis began crafting marriage covenants—Ketubahs—beautifully written promises outlining the husband's devotion to protect and cherish his bride. This isn't just an ancient tradition; it's a powerful symbol that echoes back to Mount Sinai. As we stood there, this very concept came to life for our group—a living memorial to the holy covenant we had made with Yehovah, binding us together in faith and purpose.

The Unexpected Event

Let me take you right into this unforgettable moment: it was the final day of our expedition—a Tuesday—when fifteen of us set out, hearts pounding, to climb to the very altar built by Moses at Mount Sinai. Imagine the scene: two photographers capturing every sacred detail, one man standing ready to officiate, and, by what felt like divine orchestration, twelve witnesses gathered at the altar—just as twelve tribes once stood before Yehovah. None of us had planned it that way, but the symbolism was striking and awe-inspiring.

As we completed the covenant and shared the meal in remembrance of Yeshua, something miraculous happened. A cloud began to swirl around the dark peak of Sinai, and suddenly a powerful storm broke loose. Hail pelted the ground—so much that it looked like manna scattered at our feet. The rain continued to fall all day, drenching the mountain in mystery. And later, to our amazement, snow began to fall, blanketing Mount Sinai in white. It felt as if heaven itself had joined our covenant celebration, confirming that we were seen and heard in a way we could never have imagined.

In that breathtaking moment, my husband David recalled the words from Exodus 19, which describe the original covenant at Sinai:

> Then it came to pass on the third day, in the morning, that there were thunderings and lightnings, and a thick cloud on the mountain... Now Mount Sinai [was] completely in smoke, because Yehovah descended upon it in fire. Its smoke ascended like the smoke of a furnace... Exodus 19:1-9, 16, 18

With our hearts full of hope, we prayed—asking Yehovah for a sign, a confirmation that our covenant promise reached His ears. Incredibly, Yehovah answered with a miracle that left us in awe! That's why I'm so excited to share this Mount Sinai miracle blessing with you, a fellow seeker and servant of Yehovah.

If you feel stirred to make a covenant with Yehovah, I invite you to take these meaningful steps:

- Prepare your heart. Quiet yourself and open up to Him. Confess your disobedience and ask for forgiveness in the name of Yeshua, letting His grace wash over you.
- Repent—let your heart and mind be transformed so you're willing to do all He asks, including making amends with anyone you may have harmed.
- Read aloud—on your own or with loved ones—the words of the covenant below, letting them sink into your soul.

- Confirm your commitment by sharing the bread and wine (or grape juice) in remembrance of Yeshua and the incredible sacrifice He made for you.

As you walk through these steps, know that you're not just performing a ritual—you're stepping into a living legacy, connecting yourself to the miraculous story of Mount Sinai. This blessing is for you as well. Will you say yes to the journey?

Ketubah of The Covenant at Mount Sinai

A Ketubah Covenant (written marriage covenant) on this ______ day of ______ in the year ________, Yehovah and ________________________ have entered into a covenant as one with Yehovah and His Son, Yeshua the Messiah (John 17:21), and now I am part of the children of Israel and agree to the following words:

(READ THE FOLLOWING VERSES ALOUD)

And now, come, I am sending you to Pharaoh, to bring My people, the children of Yisra'ěl, out of Mitsrayim. And Mosheh said to Elohim, "Who am I that I should go to Pharaoh, and that I should bring the children of Yisra'ěl out of Mitsrayim?' And He said, 'Because I am with you. And this is to you the sign that I have sent you: When you have brought the people out of Mitsrayim, you are to serve Elohim on this mountain.' And Mosheh said to Elohim, 'See, when I come to the children of Yisra'ěl and say to them, 'The Elohim of your fathers has sent me to you,' and they say to me, 'What is His Name?' what shall I say to them?' And Elohim said to Mosheh, 'I am that which I am.' And He said, 'Thus you shall say to the children of Yisra'ěl, 'I am has sent me to you.' And Elohim said further to Mosheh, 'Thus you are to say to the children of Yisra'ěl, 'יהוה Elohim of your fathers, the Elohim of Aḇraham, the Elohim of Yitsḥaq, and the Elohim of Ya'aqoḇ, has sent me to you. **This is My Name forever, and this is My remembrance to all generations.**' Exodus 3:10-15 ISR (emphasis mine)

And Mosheh went up to Elohim, and יהוה called to him from the mountain, saying, "This is what you are to say to the house of Ya'aqoḇ, and declare to the children of Yisra'ěl: 'You have seen what I did to the Mitsrites, and how I bore you on eagles' wings and brought you to Myself. And now, if you diligently obey My voice, and shall guard My covenant, then you shall be My treasured possession above all the peoples – for all the earth is Mine – and you shall be to Me a reign of priests and a set-apart nation.' Those are the words which you are to speak to the children of Yisra'ĕl.' And Mosheh came and called for the elders of the people, and set before them all these words which יהוה commanded him. And all the people answered together and said, '**All that יהוה has spoken we shall do**.' So Mosheh brought back the words of the people to יהוה. Exodus 19:8 ISR (emphasis mine)

And Mosheh went up to Elohim, and יהוה called to him from the mountain, saying, This is what you are to say to the house of Ya'aqoḇ, and declare to the children of Yisra'ĕl: 'You have seen what I did to the Mitsrites, and how I bore you on eagles' wings and brought you to Myself. And now, if you diligently obey My voice, and shall guard My covenant, then you shall be My treasured possession above all the peoples – for all the earth is Mine – and you shall be to Me a reign of priests and a set-apart nation.' Those are the words which you are to speak to the children of Yisra'ĕl.' And Mosheh came and called for the elders of the people, and set before them all these words which יהוה commanded him. And all the people answered together and said, "**All that יהוה has spoken we shall do**." So Mosheh brought back the words of the people to יהוה. Exodus 19:3-8, ISR (emphasis mine)

See, I am sending a Messenger before you to guard you in the way and to bring you into the place which I have prepared. Be on guard before Him and obey His voice. Do not rebel against Him, for He is not going to pardon your transgression, for My Name is in Him. But if you diligently obey His voice and shall do all that I speak, then I shall be an enemy to your enemies and a distresser to those who distress you. Exodus 23:20-22, ISR

And you shall serve יהוה your Elohim, and He shall bless your bread and your water. And I shall remove sickness from your midst. None shall miscarry or be barren in your land. I shall fill the number of your days. I shall send My fear before you, and cause confusion among all the people to whom you come, and make all your enemies turn their backs to you. And I shall send hornets before you, which shall drive out the Ḥiwwite, the Kenaʽanite, and the Ḥittite from before you. Exodus 23:25-28 ISR

And Mosheh came and related to the people all the Words of יהוה and all the right-rulings. And all the people answered with one voice and said, '**All the Words which יהוה has spoken we shall do**.' Exodus 24:3, ISR (emphasis mine)

And Mosheh came and related to the people all the Words of יהוה and all the right-rulings. And all the people answered with one voice and said, "All the Words which יהוה has spoken we shall do.' And Mosheh wrote down all the Words of יהוה, and rose up early in the morning, and built a slaughter-place at the foot of the mountain, and twelve standing columns for the twelve tribes of Yisra'ěl. And he sent young men of the children of Yisra'ěl, and they offered ascending offerings and slaughtered slaughterings of peace offerings to יהוה of bulls. And Mosheh took half the blood and put it in basins, and half the blood he sprinkled on the slaughter-place. And he took the Book of the Covenant and read in the hearing of the people. And they said, '**All that יהוה has spoken we shall do, and obey.**' And Mosheh took the blood and sprinkled it on the people, and said, 'See, the blood of the covenant which יהוה has made with you concerning all these Words.' Exodus 24:3-8, ISR (emphasis mine)

And it came to be, on the third day in the morning, that there were thunders and lightnings, and a thick cloud on the mountain. And a voice of a shophar was very strong, and all the people who were in the camp trembled. (Exodus 19:16, ISR)

All of you are standing today before יהוה your Elohim: your leaders, your tribes, your elders and your officers, all the men of Yisra'ěl, your little ones, your wives, and your sojourner who is in the midst of your

> camp, from the one who cuts your wood to the one who draws your water,so that you should enter into covenant with יהוה your Elohim, and into His oath, which יהוה your Elohim makes with you today, in order to establish you today as a people for Himself, and He Himself be your Elohim, as He has spoken to you, and as He has sworn to your fathers, to Aḇraham, to Yitsḥaq, and to Ya'aqoḇ. **And not with you alone I am making this covenant and this oath,' but with him who stands here with us today before יהוה our Elohim, as well as with him who is not here with us today**. (Deuteronomy 29:11-15, ISR, emphasis mine)

Today, I made a vow to Yehovah according to His blood covenant described in Exodus 19 – 24. I am sealed in the blood of Yeshua, my redeemer, and I am one with Yehovah and His begotten Son, Yeshua (John 17:21).

I agree with the terms of this covenant: **"All that Yehovah has spoken, I shall do and obey! I shall serve Yehovah and keep His covenant."**

In return for our obedience, Yehovah has agreed to do the following:

1. I am part of a special people set apart unto Yehovah above all peoples. (Exodus 3:10-15)
2. I am part of the kingdom of priests and a holy nation unto Yehovah. (Exodus 3:10-15)
3. An angel is sent before us who will be an enemy to our enemies and an adversary to our adversaries. (Ex 23:20-22)
4. Yehovah shall bless our bread and our water. He will take sickness from our midst. (Exodus 23:25-28)
5. We shall not suffer miscarriage or be barren in our land. (Exodus 23:25-28)
6. Our days will be fulfilled. (Exodus 23:25-28)
7. Yehovah will send fear before us among our enemies and cause confusion among the people whom we encounter. He will drive out our enemies. In addition, all the blessings of Deuteronomy chapter 28:1-14.

Signature: ____________________ Date: _________

Witness #1: ____________________ Date: __________

Witness #2: ____________________ Date: __________

Bibliography

Baca, Janice F. 2024. *Demons, Devils, Deities: And The Four Witnesses*. Hondo, Texas.

Baca, Janice. 2024. *The Scroll of Mysteries: Cochin Hebrew Revelation*. Second Edition. Hondo, Texas.

British Royal Museum in London, Royal MS 16 A II.

Brooke, George J. "Power to the Powerless—A Long-Lost Song of Miriam," *Biblical Archaeology Review* 20 (1994): 62–65. The Miriam fragment is published in Sidnie A. White, "4Q364 and 365: A Preliminary Report," in The Madrid Qumran Conference, eds. J. Trebolle Barrera and L. Vegas Montaner, Studies in the Text of the Desert of Judah 11 (Leiden: Brill; Madrid: Editorial Complutense, 1992).

Brown, Francis, S R Driver, Charles A Briggs, Edward Robinson, James Strong, and Wilhelm Gesenius. 2015. *The Brown, Driver, Briggs Hebrew and English Lexicon: With an Appendix Containing the Biblical Aramaic: Coded with the Numbering System from Strong's Exhaustive Concordance of the Bible*. Peabody, Mass.: Hendrickson Publishers.

Chaim Bentorah. 2023. "Hebrew Word Study – a Pruning Praise – Zamar - Chaim Bentorah." Chaim Bentorah. April 5, 2023. https://www.chaimbentorah.com/2023/04/hebrew-word-study-a-pruning-praise-zamar/.

"DigiVatLib." 2025. Vatlib.it. 2025. https://digi.vatlib.it/view/MSS_Vat.ebr.100/0007.

Fritz, C.E. 2017. "Psalms, Hymns, or Spiritual Songs?: A Millennial's Journey with the Worship Wars." Honours thesis: Southeastern University

G Johannes Botterweck, and Helmer Ringgren. 1980. *Theological Dictionary of the Old Testament*. Grand Rapids, Mich.: William B. Eerdmans Pub. Co. See link for a free download all 17 vols: https://archive.org/details/theological-dictionary-of-the-old-testament/Theological%20Dictionary%20of%20the%20Old%20Testament%20-%2001/.

Hames, Harvey J. 2012. "Translated from Catalan: Looking at a Fifteenth-Century Hebrew Version of the Gospels," January, 285–302.

Jones, M. 2021. *The Epistle of James (Ya'akov): A Translation from the Hebrew*. Edited by Pam Lutzker and Jonathan Felt. Kerrville, Texas: B'nai Emunah Institute for Accelerated Learning.

Joüon, Paul, and Takamitsu Muraoka. 2005. *A Grammar of Biblical Hebrew*. Roma: Ed. Pontificio Istituto Biblico.

Ludwig Köhler, and Walter Baumgartner. 2001. *The Hebrew and Aramaic Lexicon of the Old Testament*. Hebrew and Aramaic in contact. In: R. Hasselbach-Andee (Ed.), A companion to Ancient Near Eastern languages. Blackwell.

Malloch, S. and Trevarthen, C. 2018. "The Human Nature of Music." Frontiers in Psychology 9:1680.

Municipal Archives of Marseille, Marseille, France Ms. 48.

"Neues Testament in Hebräischer Übersetzung ([S. L.], 1563) (Universitätsbibliothek Freiburg I. Br., Hs. 314) - Digital Collections Freiburg - University Library Freiburg." 2025. Uni-Freiburg.de. 2025. https://dl.ub.uni-freiburg.de/diglit/hs314?ui_lang=eng.

"Paris. Bibliothèque Sainte-Geneviève, Ms. 131 | Biblissima." 2025. Biblissima.fr. 2025. Website: https://portail.biblissima.fr/en/ark:/43093/mdata62ef2966f5fc2ec579d00a3175d46415cad214d0.

Smith, Timothy. 2019. "Review of The Piel Stem System." River Valley Conference of the Minnesota District, February 2019, 6-8.

Wilhelm Gesenius and Samuel Prideaux Tregelles. 1979. *Gesenius' Hebrew and Chaldee Lexicon to the Old Testament Scriptures*. Grand Rapids, Mich.: Baker Book House. Copyright.

Yende, S.J. and Moshugi, K.S. 2024. "Gospel Music As an Intervention for Peace and Social Change in South Africa." International Journal of Religion 5(11):5192–5200.

Discover More Exciting Books by Janice F Baca!

Janice F Baca unveils astonishing secrets hidden within *The Scroll of Mysteries: Cochin Hebrew Revelation*, linking them back to Ezekiel 9 and the ancient legendary Song of the Sea described in Exodus 15—a war song that was the first song and will become the last song at the end of the ages. She reimagines this renewed power-of-God song sung by the 144,000, restoring long-lost verses from the Qumran Caves that have been partially preserved for generations. These verses will be fully restored when Yeshua teaches them their song that no one else can learn. Most remarkably, she reveals, through Hebrew grammatical insights, who the 144,000 truly are: men, women, and children from both the past and the present! These chosen ones will be summoned to Jerusalem for their sealing for the Biblical feast day of the Day of Atonement, as Messiah Yeshua arrives from the Eastern gate, holding the seal in His hand, ready to claim them as His own!

Discover More Exciting Books by Janice F Baca!

Discover Janice F. Baca's remarkable book, *Demons, Devils, Deities: And the Four Witnesses*, and explore the deep mysteries revealed in these final days through the Song of Moses. As tormenting dreams and demonic influences rise and destroy lives, darkness persists relentlessly, whether by day or night, offering little hope for relief. But there is hope—a prophecy. The prophecy given by Moses is unfolding before our eyes in these latter days, as described in the Song of Moses. Moses warned us about this very day, and now that day has arrived. The key to victory is simple and certain—find out what it is.

Discover More Exciting Books by Janice F Baca!

The Scroll of Mysteries: Cochin Hebrew Revelation (Cambridge MS Oo.1.16.2) is an extraordinary translation of a unique Hebrew Revelation uncovered in Cochin, India, in 1803 by Claudius Buchanan within the synagogue of the Malabari Black Jews. Currently housed in the Cambridge University Library in the UK, this rare manuscript is imbued with late Second Temple Hebrew grammatical markers, as tradition suggests. The Cochin Hebrew Revelation offers not only an English translation but also stunning manuscript images, detailed transcription, and interlinear tables for passionate researchers. You can also find a free download available on ProjectTruthMinistries.org.

www.ingramcontent.com/pod-product-compliance
Lightning Source LLC
LaVergne TN
LVHW010545100826
845148LV00013B/2615